EARTH'S UNDERGROUND STRUCTURES

Heather C. Hudak

CRABTREE
PUBLISHING COMPANY
WWW.CRABTREEBOOKS.COM

CRABTREE
PUBLISHING COMPANY
WWW.CRABTREEBOOKS.COM

Author: Heather C. Hudak

Editorial Director: Kathy Middleton

Editors: Petrice Custance, Sonya Newland

Proofreaders: Lorna Notsch, Ellen Rodger

Designer: Steve Mead

Cover design: Tammy McGarr

Production coordinator and
Prepress technician: Tammy McGarr

Print coordinator: Katherine Berti

Produced for Crabtree Publishing Company
by White-Thomson Publishing Ltd

Photographs

Cover: iStock: Berti123 (top right)

Interior: Alamy: 9 (Poelzer Wolfgang), 13 (Steve Taylor APRS), 15 (age footstock), 17 (Kim Karpeles), 25 (Frans Lanting Studio), 29 (Zachary Frank); Julian Baker: 6, 21, 22; Getty Images: 12 (Romeo Gacad); iStock: 18–19 (Onfokus); NASA: 16 (JPL/NGA); NOAA: 26, 27; Shutterstock: 4 (CurryPuff_Studio16), 5 (Marcus Bay), 7 (Zarnell Photography), 8 (Israel Hervas Bengochea), 10 (NelzTabcharani316), 11 (Aleksandar Todorovic), 14 (Nido Huebl), 19 (Lakeview Images), 20 (Vladi333), 23 (Edward Fielding), 24–25 (Lynn Yeh), 28 (jiawangkun).

Library and Archives Canada Cataloguing in Publication

Hudak, Heather C., 1975-, author
      Earth's underground structures / Heather C. Hudak.

(Underground worlds)
Includes index.
Issued in print and electronic formats.
ISBN 978-0-7787-6079-5 (hardcover).--ISBN 978-0-7787-6129-7 (softcover).--ISBN 978-1-4271-2248-3 (HTML)

      1. Geodynamics--Juvenile literature. 2. Geology, Structural--Juvenile literature. 3. Caves--Juvenile literature. 4. Faults (Geology)--Juvenile literature. 5. Landforms--Juvenile literature. I. Title.

QE501.25.H83 2018   j551.44   C2018-905524-3
                                                        C2018-905525-1

Library of Congress Cataloging-in-Publication Data

Names: Hudak, Heather C., 1975- author.
Title: Earth's underground structures / Heather C. Hudak.
Description: New York, NY : Crabtree Publishing, [2019] |
   Series: Underground worlds | Includes index.
Identifiers: LCCN 2018043796 (print) | LCCN 2018047221 (ebook) |
   ISBN 9781427122483 (Electronic) |
   ISBN 9780778760795 (hardcover) |
   ISBN 9780778761297 (pbk.)
Subjects: LCSH: Geodynamics--Juvenile literature. | Geology,
   Structural--Juvenile literature. | Caves--Juvenile literature. | Faults
   (Geology)--Juvenile literature. | Landforms--Juvenile literature.
Classification: LCC QE501.25 (ebook) | LCC QE501.25 .H83 2019 (print) |
   DDC   551.44--dc23
LC record available at https://lccn.loc.gov/2018043796

Crabtree Publishing Company

www.crabtreebooks.com   1-800-387-7650

Printed in the U.S.A./122018/CG20181005

Published in Canada
Crabtree Publishing
616 Welland Ave.
St. Catharines, Ontario
L2M 5V6

Published in the United States
Crabtree Publishing
PMB 59051
350 Fifth Avenue, 59th Floor
New York, New York 10118

Published in the United Kingdom
Crabtree Publishing
Maritime House
Basin Road North, Hove
BN41 1WR

Published in Australia
Crabtree Publishing
3 Charles Street
Coburg North
VIC, 3058

CONTENTS

BENEATH THE SURFACE

Look around you—what do you see? Are there mountains rising into the sky? Crystal blue waters filled with fish? Earth's surface is covered with stunning scenery. But did you know there are also spectacular natural structures beneath Earth's surface?

Underground Features

Caves, volcanoes, rivers, and oceans are just a few of the features hidden from view beneath the surface of our planet. Humans had no part in making these structures—they were designed by nature. Since the beginning of time, natural events have created and shaped many underground **landforms** around the world.

▽ There are more than 5,000 active underwater volcanoes on Earth.

DID YOU KNOW?

The largest underwater volcano is Kolumbo on the island of Santorini in Greece. It last erupted in 1650. The blast was felt 93 miles (150 km) away.

Nature's Architects

Caves form when rainwater seeps through **decomposing** plants in the soil. This causes the rainwater to become **acidic**. Over thousands of years, the acidic rainwater eats away at rocks, forming caves. Other underground structures form when **tectonic plates** shift and collide. When two plates hit each other hard, one rises above the other, and underwater volcanoes or **rift valleys** can form.

Deep Discoveries

Some underground structures are discovered by accident by people who are exploring new areas. Others are detected using cutting-edge technologies such as underwater robots. Scientists use special equipment to take photographs and create maps of structures that cannot be seen aboveground. Today, many of these discoveries are popular tourist attractions.

▽ Some caves fill with water. Activities such as cave diving allow people to see the incredible natural scenery that lies below Earth's surface.

HANG SON DOONG

The lush forest and rocky landscape in Phong Nha-Ke Bang National Park in Vietnam give us a sense of what the world was like when dinosaurs roamed the land. This is home to Hang Son Doong—the world's biggest cave.

▽ Some features of the Hang Son Doong cave have been given unusual names.

Garden of Edam

Great Wall of Vietnam

Passchendaele

Watch Out for Dinosaurs (**sinkhole**)

Fossil passage

Deep Dive

The cave formed between two and five million years ago, when river water wore away the **limestone** beneath the ground. At first, researchers thought the cave was only 200 feet (60 m) high and 500 feet (150 m) long. In fact, it is three times as high and more than 3 miles (5 km) long. Hang Son Doong is part of a network of more than 150 caves.

△ Hang Son Doong is so big that it has its own weather system! Rain clouds can form inside the cave.

Cave entrance

Take a Tour

The cave was discovered by a local farmer in 1991. He told a group of British **cavers** working nearby about the cave, but he could not remember how to get back to it. He finally found it again in 2009.

Tourism has brought jobs for people who live near the cave. However, Hang Son Doong is part of a unique and fragile **ecosystem**, so it is important to protect it from damage. Only a few hundred tourists are allowed to visit Hang Son Doong each year. Visitors camp inside the cave. They must crawl, climb, and swim to explore the cave network.

MID-ATLANTIC RIDGE

Did you know there is an underwater mountain range that stretches 10,000 miles (16,000 km) from the southern tip of Africa all the way to Iceland? It is made up of a chain of mid-ocean ridges (underwater mountains) that form the longest mountain range in the world.

Ancient Range

The Mid-Atlantic Ridge formed 195–225 million years ago. However, it was only discovered in the 1870s. A group of scientists was looking for the best place to lay a transatlantic **telegraph** cable when they noticed a ridge in the middle of the Atlantic Ocean. Their discovery was confirmed using **sonar** in 1925.

In the 1950s, scientists began mapping the Mid-Atlantic Ridge. They learned it was part of a much larger mountain chain that runs 24,855 miles (40,000 km) along the floor of every ocean on Earth.

▽ The top of the Mid-Atlantic Ridge runs through a national park in Iceland.

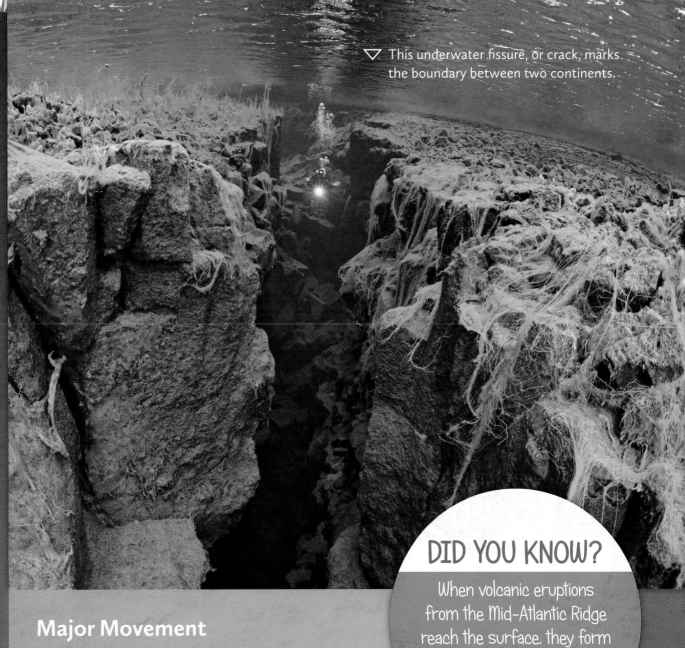

▽ This underwater fissure, or crack, marks the boundary between two continents.

Major Movement

A huge rift valley runs the entire length of the Mid-Atlantic Ridge. It separates the North American tectonic plate from the Eurasian plate, and the South American plate from the African plate. At the edges of the plates, **magma** from inside Earth rises to the seafloor. This process is known as "seafloor spreading," and it pushes the plates apart. The Atlantic Ocean is widening at a rate of approximately 0.5–4 inches (1–10 cm) each year.

DID YOU KNOW?

When volcanic eruptions from the Mid-Atlantic Ridge reach the surface, they form islands, such as Iceland. A new island formed in 1963, called Surtsey.

PUERTO PRINCESA
UNDERGROUND RIVER

Deep beneath the island of Palawan in the Philippines flows the second-longest underground river in the world. Puerto Princesa Underground River stretches for more than 5 miles (8.2 km).

Stony Secret

The only way to access Puerto Princesa Underground River is through a stone cliff that is partly underwater. From the outside, it is impossible to tell the beauty that lies on the other side of the cliff wall. Once inside, visitors can travel 2.7 miles (4.3 km) of the river through caves with unique rock formations, such as **stalagmites** and **stalactites**.

There are some amazing formations along the river, created by a build-up of **minerals** and water wearing away the rock. ▷

▽ Many companies organize boat trips along the underground river.

Second Story

In 2010, a group of scientists discovered many small waterfalls inside the cave and realized that the river had a second level. They also found a massive cave dome that reached 980 feet (300 m) above the underground river. But that was not all. Large bats and sea animals had made their home there. There were also river **channels**, another huge cave, and more! Scientists cannot explore any deeper into the river due to a lack of oxygen.

DID YOU KNOW?

Some of the rock formations at Puerto Princesa look like mushrooms, a horse, and religious figures.

Precious Park

The river is part of Puerto Princesa Subterranean River National Park. In 1999, the park was named a **UNESCO World Heritage Site**. In 2012, millions of people voted to include the park on a list called the New7Wonders of Nature. The places on this list are known as the seven most spectacular natural landscapes on Earth.

To help conserve the area, only 600 visitors a day are permitted in the national park.

Special Species

The national park is known for its vast **biodiversity**. It is home to more than 800 plant species and some of the most important forests in Asia. There are 165 kinds of birds, 30 mammal species, and 19 types of reptiles living in the park. Many different creatures live in the underground river and cave system. Some of them are not found anywhere else on Earth. Others are endangered or are very rare. All these creatures have adapted to living underground.

Swallows, swiftlets, and eight species of bats live inside the cave and its chambers. They use sonar to navigate the darkness. Mygalomorph spiders, cave crickets, giant centipedes, snakes, lizards, and tailless whip scorpions are also found within the river system. The water itself contains a variety of fish—including catfish and black mouth croaker—and creatures such as shrimp.

DID YOU KNOW?

Scientists found the 20-million-year-old fossil of a sea cow in the cave walls above the Puerto Princesa Underground River. The fossil was in perfect condition. It was the first fossil of this type of species found in the area.

△ Birds such as swiftlets nest in cave entrances.

SISTEMA SAC ACTUN

Near the town of Tulum in the Yucatán Peninsula of Mexico lies the world's largest underwater cave—Sistema Sac Actun. Sac Actun, the longest underground river in the world, runs through the system.

Ancient Origins

Scientists believe the caves formed when a **comet** fell to Earth 65 million years ago. The comet left a huge crater in the Gulf of Mexico, more than 112 miles (180 km) around and 12 miles (20 km) deep. Cracks and holes made by the comet filled with rainwater and became caves and rivers.

Amazing stalagmites ▷ and stalactites can be seen throughout Sistema Sac Actun.

Cave divers are always ▷ finding new parts of the Sistema Sac Actun.

Sacred Site

Sistema Sac Actun is Mayan for "White Cave System." The cave was a sacred place for the Mayan peoples. They believed the souls of the dead used the river inside the cave system as a gateway to the afterlife. Human skulls and religious objects have been found at the bottom of some of the sinkholes inside the cave.

And the Winner Is...

For years, Sistema Sac Actun competed with Sistema Ox Bel Ha in eastern Mexico for the title of longest underwater cave system. In 2018, divers learned that Sistema Sac Actun was connected to another cave system, called Dos Ojos. Together, they span 216 miles (347 km). Sistema Ox Bel Ha is only 168 miles (270 km).

ALPINE FAULT

Alpine **Fault** in New Zealand is a major tectonic plate boundary. The fault lies where the Pacific and Australian plates meet. This is one of the most dangerous earthquake zones in New Zealand!

Miles and Miles

Alpine Fault is hidden deep underground. It spans more than 500 miles (800 km) of New Zealand's South Island. When the first European settlers arrived in the 1840s, they did not know the fault was there. They began building homes in the area, which grew into towns and cities. In the mid-1900s, two scientists were mapping the area when they discovered the fault. By then, it was too late to warn people not to settle nearby.

▽ This radar image shows the Alpine Fault (the area in darker green) running along the west coast of New Zealand's South Island.

The Franz Josef Glacier runs down the western side of the Southern Alps into the region of the Alpine Fault.

Rising Up

Scientists have tracked ruptures, or splits, in the Alpine Fault as far back as 8,000 years. They use new technologies to date seeds, leaves, and reeds found at 24 rupture zones along the fault. In the past 900 years, the Alpine Fault has ruptured four times. The ruptures took place in approximately the years 1100, 1450, 1620, and 1717.

Evidence of faults can sometimes be seen aboveground. As a fault ruptures, rock is pushed up, creating landforms such as mountains. The Alpine Fault runs along a mountain range called the Southern Alps. Each time the Alpine Fault ruptures, it lifts the mountains a little higher. The range has risen about 12 miles (20 km) in the past 12 million years. However, **erosion** wears down the mountains and keeps them from getting higher overall.

17

Danger Zone

The Alpine Fault ruptures about every 230 years. It is expected to rupture again within the next few decades. When it does, it may create a huge earthquake. This could be disastrous for people living in the earthquake zone. In a matter of minutes, glass will shatter, roads will be buried, buildings will crumble, and power lines will fall. Local authorities are working on an emergency plan to help prepare for an earthquake.

Digging Deep

The Deep Fault Drilling Project is a major project along part of the Alpine Fault near the community of Whataroa, New Zealand. Scientists hope to learn how large faults such as the Alpine Fault change over time. They have taken rock and fluid samples, and made measurements of the fault.

▽ New Zealand experiences up to 150 earthquakes a year that are large enough to be felt. Some cause severe damage, as seen below.

As part of the project, scientists drilled a hole 3,000 feet (914 m) into the fault line. The temperature inside the hole was much hotter than normal. Water at the bottom of the hole was boiling hot. Now the scientists are looking for ways to use the site as a **geothermal energy** source for local communities and industries.

DFDP Investigating the Alpine Fault at depth

All visitors please report to the site office on arrival

alpine.icdp-online.org
Ph: 021 127 1012 or 027 273 1

△ Instruments have been placed inside the fault to monitor activity inside it.

DID YOU KNOW?

Tectonic plates at Alpine Fault are constantly moving. They change the position of the fault at a rate of about 98 feet (30 m) from left to right every 1,000 years.

SUBTERRANEAN SEA

Scientists have found what may be the largest water **reservoir** on the planet! It is more than 400 miles (645 km) beneath Earth's **crust**.

Solving the Puzzle

For years, experts have wondered where the water on Earth's surface came from. Some think it may have come from ice-covered comets that smashed into Earth. Others think it came from deep inside the planet. Thanks to the discovery of water in Earth's **core** beneath North America, scientists are getting closer to the truth.

◁ One theory is that comets containing water molecules crashed into Earth billions of years ago.

Water World

Scientists discovered what may be an underground ocean while studying the speed of **seismic waves**. Experts can tell what types of rocks are inside Earth by measuring how fast seismic waves travel. It takes longer for the waves to pass through wet rock than dry rock. When the waves slowed down, the scientists knew they had found signs of wet rock.

The water is trapped inside a blue rock called ringwoodite. It is found at a point deep inside Earth where the pressure and temperature are just right to squeeze water out of the rock—almost like sweating! Scientists believe some of the water inside the rock may have oozed to Earth's surface to fill the oceans.

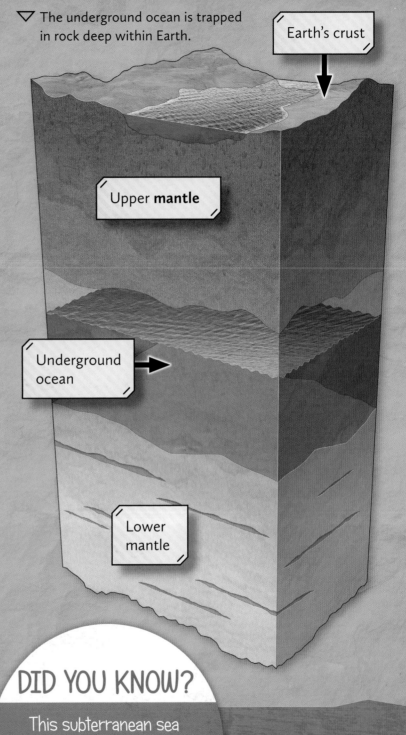

▽ The underground ocean is trapped in rock deep within Earth.

Earth's crust

Upper **mantle**

Underground ocean

Lower mantle

DID YOU KNOW?

This subterranean sea could contain more than three times as much water as all of Earth's oceans combined!

YELLOWSTONE
VOLCANO

Yellowstone National Park sits on top of a supervolcano, which is thousands of times bigger than a regular volcano. A supervolcano eruption would be devastating. The gas ejected could cause changes to climates around the world.

Heated History

The volcano at Yellowstone first erupted approximately 2.1 million years ago. It shot 600 cubic miles (2,500 cu km) of rock and ash into the air. That is about the same as the amount of water that flows through Niagara Falls in four months!

Super-eruptions took place again 1.2 million years ago and 640,000 years ago. Each time, they caused huge amounts of destruction across the planet. Ash would have filled the air over most of the United States for weeks.

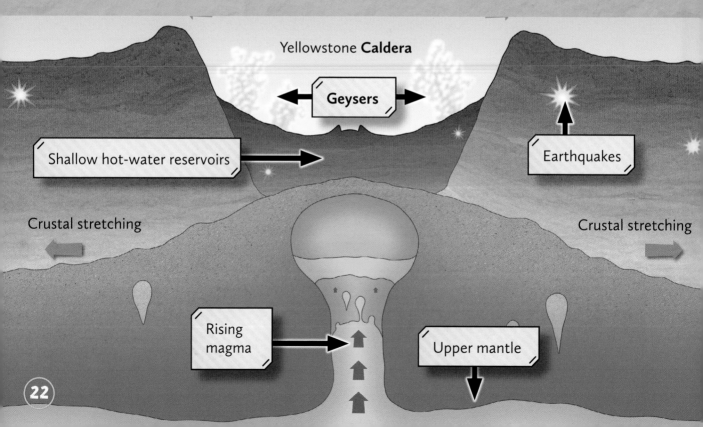

Yellowstone **Caldera**

Geysers

Shallow hot-water reservoirs

Earthquakes

Crustal stretching

Crustal stretching

Rising magma

Upper mantle

Park Perks

During the Yellowstone supervolcano's last major eruption 640,000 years ago, part of the volcano caved in on itself. It created the giant Yellowstone Caldera, which covers 1,500 square miles (3,885 sq km) of Yellowstone National Park. Yellowstone Lake also formed during this time.

We cannot see the supervolcano that lies beneath Yellowstone. However, the park's bubbling geysers and hot springs give us clues about the heat and magma brewing underground. Hundreds of tiny earthquakes shake the park each year.

▽ Yellowstone National Park contains about half of all the known geysers in the world. This is one of the most famous, nicknamed "Old Faithful."

DID YOU KNOW?

There are more than 300 geysers in Yellowstone National Park. Many shoot water more than 100 feet (30 m) into the air.

Looking Ahead

Thanks to modern technology, scientists can detect volcanic eruptions weeks, months, or even years in advance. They use tools such as satellites and radar to monitor underground activity. Scientists have been watching the supervolcano at Yellowstone for more than 30 years. They do not think it will erupt within the next 10,000 years. In fact, no one knows for sure if it will ever erupt again.

▽ Bubbling hot springs in Yellowstone National Park are signs of supervolcano activity underground.

△ Researchers study the activity in the hot springs and geysers to predict what is going on deep underground.

Slowing the Flow

Scientists think they have found a way to help prevent an eruption at Yellowstone in the future. They want to slow the flow of moving lava beneath the park. When magma is molten, or in liquid form, it has a higher chance of erupting. Scientists plan to drill into the supervolcano's magma chambers and pipe in cold water to release heat. This will help cool the magma and keep it from becoming molten.

DID YOU KNOW?

If the supervolcano at Yellowstone erupts, it would probably cause more damage than an asteroid colliding with Earth.

WEST MATA VOLCANO

About 80 percent of all volcanic eruptions take place deep underwater on the ocean floor. They are almost impossible to find or see. But a few years ago, scientists caught a lucky break.

Active Area

The West Mata Volcano is located in the Pacific Ocean, about 124 miles (200 km) southwest of Samoa, between the islands of Fiji and Tonga. The volcano is 6 miles (9.7 km) long, 4 miles (6.4 km) wide, and rises 1 mile (1.6 km) from the seafloor. West Mata is one of 452 volcanoes in an area of volcanic activity known as the **Pacific Ring of Fire**.

◁ The top of the volcano lies 4,000 feet (1,219 m) below the surface of the Pacific Ocean.

Scientists discovered water-rich lava called boninite at the site. Until then, they had only seen this type of lava at extinct volcanoes more than one million years old.

DID YOU KNOW?

Some sea animals, such as shrimp, thrive in the acidic waters around West Mata. Scientists are looking at whether some species are unique to the area and how they can live in such harsh conditions.

Underwater Eruption

In 2009, an underwater robot recorded a video of the West Mata Volcano as it erupted at the bottom of the ocean. At 2,200 feet (670 m) underwater, the West Mata eruption is the deepest ever recorded. Scientists had never seen anything like it before. In fact, they did not think volcanoes could erupt at that depth! Molten lava bubbles from West Mata measured 3 feet (1 m) across. The lava burst through the cold seawater, cooling and creating a black rock that sank to the ocean floor.

MAMMOTH CAVE
NATIONAL PARK

Beneath the forests, rivers, and hills of Mammoth Cave National Park in Kentucky, USA, lies an extensive network of limestone caves. To date, 400 miles (650 km) of underground passages have been explored—and more are being discovered all the time.

Ancient History

Scientists have found the remains of **Indigenous** peoples inside Mammoth Cave. Their bodies were preserved by the cool, dry air and unique soil found there.

Around 4,000 years ago, Indigenous peoples began exploring more than 6 miles (9.6 km) of Mammoth Cave.

They mined several types of minerals. They left behind thousands of artifacts, such as pottery, rock paintings, and cloth, which tell us about their daily lives. Then, about 2,000 years ago, all signs of life vanished. The cave remained untouched by humans for 2,300 years.

▽ Inside, visitors can see evidence of early humans, as well as stalagmites, stalactites, lakes, and rivers.

Keeping Connected

In 1972, a passage was found that linked Mammoth Cave to another cave within the park—the Flint Ridge Cave System. Eleven years later, Roppel Cave was discovered to the east of the park. These three caves, along with many other caves and passages, combine to make Mammoth the world's longest system of connected caves.

△ The Flint Ridge Cave System forms an extension of Mammoth Caves.

DID YOU KNOW?

Nitrate was mined from the cave to make gunpowder during the War of 1812. Later, the cave was used as a hospital for people suffering from **tuberculosis**.

GLOSSARY

acidic Describes something that can dissolve a material

biodiversity The variety of plant and animal life in a particular area

caldera A large crater created when a volcano erupts

caver Someone who explores caves for research or for fun

channel A ditch or groove that water runs through

comet A chunk of ice and dust that travels around the Sun

core The very middle part of Earth; the inner core is solid metal while the outer core is liquid metal

crust The hard, rocky, outer layer of Earth

decomposing Decaying, or rotting

ecosystem All the plants and animals that live in a particular area, and the natural features of that area

erosion Wearing away by wind, water, and other natural elements

fault A crack in Earth's crust caused by the movement of tectonic plates

geothermal energy Energy from heat stored inside Earth

geyser A pool of hot water that sometimes erupts in a jet of water and steam

Indigenous Describes people who originally lived in a particular region

landform A nature feature found on Earth

limestone A type of soft rock

magma Liquid rock formed by heat inside Earth

mantle The layer of Earth between the crust, near the surface, and the core in the middle

mineral A substance formed naturally in the earth

Pacific Ring of Fire An area of volcanic activity that stretches along the South and North American coastlines, across the Bering Strait, and from Japan to New Zealand

reservoir A large store of water

rift valley A low-lying area between mountains or highlands, formed by a fault

seismic waves Waves of energy that travel through Earth's layers during an earthquake or explosion

sinkhole A hole in the ground caused by water erosion

sonar A device that detects objects underwater by sending out sound-wave pulses that bounce off the objects and back to the device

stalactite An icicle-like structure made from mineral deposits that hangs from the roof of a cave

stalagmite A column of mineral deposits that rises up from the floor of a cave

tectonic plates Large slabs of solid rock that float and move on Earth's crust

telegraph A way of sending messages long distances using an underground wire

tuberculosis An infectious disease that affects the lungs

UNESCO World Heritage Site A place declared to have important cultural, scientific, or historic value by the United Nations Educational, Scientific, and Cultural Organization

LEARNING MORE

Books

Branley, Franklin M., *Earthquakes.* Harper Collins, 2015.

Kalman, Bobbie, *Volcanoes on Earth.* Crabtree Books, 2008.

Olson, Sonja, *Caves.* Focus Readers, 2018.

Websites

https://nature.new7wonders.com/
Learn all about the beautiful places that made the list of the New7Wonders of Nature.

www.kids-fun-science.com/yellowstone-caldera.html
Find out more about the amazing supervolcano underneath Yellowstone National Park.

INDEX